L.E.A.R.N.
EVANGELISM

PAMPHLET

1028 S Bishop Avenue, Dept. 178
Rolla, MO 65401

Printed in United States of America

L.E.A.R.N. EVANGELISM

PAMPHLET

Giving Away The Greatest Gift

Dr. Marshall M. Windsor

CHALFANT ECKERT

PUBLISHING

TABLE OF CONTENTS

A PERSONAL NOTE 6

WHAT IS L.E.A.R.N. EVANGELISM? 8

   LISTEN 9

   ENGAGE 10

   ASK 10

   RELAY 12

      SCRIPTURES 12

      WHAT DOES IT MEAN TO
      "BE SAVED?" 14

      PRAYER FOR SALVATION 16

   NEVER QUIT 16

WHAT'S NEXT? 18

MY PRAYER LIST 20

RESPONSE FORM 24

A PERSONAL NOTE

One of the scariest words in the church today is the word *evangelism*! It seems to strike fear into so many hearts and keeps us from sharing "the hope that is within" each and every follower of Jesus Christ (1 Peter 3:15). Culture today has embraced tolerance to an unhealthy level—to the point of influencing Christians to abscond from the divine directives of our Lord and Savior, Jesus Christ—to "Go therefore and make disciples of all nations" (Matthew 28:19).

Honestly, there are days when every Christian struggles with his or her inadequacies in sharing the Gospel message. Social media has only heightened the human sensitivity to insecurities and fears of rejection. No one likes to be rejected and ridiculed. As a matter of fact, evangelism in any culture demands overcoming our fears by taking a step of faith to help someone escape the coming judgment of Christ (2 Timothy 4:1). We should all pray that the love of God will so fill our hearts that we can't help but share God's wonderful news when opportunities exist. May the Lord give us a sense of holy dissatisfaction when we cease sharing what God has done in our lives and the wonderful plan that God has for His creation.

That's why I hope that this booklet will encourage you to get together with another believer or two and encourage yourselves in the Lord (1 Thess. 5:11) as you step out to scatter some Gospel seed. You can do it!

WHAT IS L.E.A.R.N. EVANGELISM?

L.E.A.R.N. evangelism is merely a tool to encourage you in starting conversations and sharing your faith. God longs to bring others into a right relationship with Him, and He may just want to use you to do that! There is no one way of sharing our faith that is fruitful in every situation; that is why the role of the Holy Spirit is so important. We all have a story about what God has done in our lives, and your story may just be *THE* story that helps change another person's life for eternity.

In this short teaching tool, I hope that the Holy Spirit will also reveal the importance of building relationships with others. Sometimes, relationships are God's teaching tools in our own lives. But truly, we need to be intentional in our relationships! The hope is to share Christ and reveal the difference He can make when a person invites Him into his or her life. So, take a deep breath, say fervent prayers for opportunities and the words to say, then step into a world waiting for you! Start building relationships and initiate discussions in hopes of sharing Christ with someone who does not know Him. Make it a point to try and make at least one new friend every year.

L.E.A.R.N. EVANGELISM MEANS TO:

LISTEN – Listen to the whisper of the Holy Spirit and to the person you encounter. As you listen, in your times of prayer or even throughout the day, you may sense the Holy Spirit nudging you to share a particular thought with a person you are with or to talk with a specific person. There are people waiting and hoping someone has answers to issues in their lives. God continues to use divine encounters if we will just listen to, and obey, the Holy Spirit's leading (John 16:13). When visiting with a person, make sure you are attentive and listening to them. This says, "I care and what *you* are saying is important."

ENGAGE – You must decide to engage another person. Many people stumble here because culture today teaches us to respect other people's privacy and to embrace tolerance. Many Christians are introverted in their social interactions, so engaging others is a challenge for them. You may prefer to engage others via a handwritten note or sending web page links to share articles or blog posts that mean a lot to you. Regardless of your preferred method, God can use that to speak to others. However, there is no better means of communication than actually talking to someone. For others who are extroverts, this is an exciting opportunity because they have never met a stranger - ever! Pray for God's peace and courage as you step out in obedience to His Word (Mark 16:15). Try starting mini-conversations with people about the weather, aspects of their jobs, or honest compliments for service. These can start conversations that end up talking about God's greatest gift.

ASK – After you decide to engage people about their faith, you must eventually ask some simple questions to help you steer the conversation toward spiritual matters. Here are some questions you might use:

- Have you ever thought about how God could bless your life?
- Is there anything special I can pray with you about?
- Have you ever, honestly, made peace with God?
- Where do you go to church?
- Have you ever thought about faith issues?
- What do think the word *salvation* means?
- Have you ever thought about eternity?
- If something terrible were to happen, do you have a peace about where you would spend eternity?

Your listening skills and the Holy Spirit will guide you in asking the right questions. Honestly, your creativity is the only limitation to the questions you can ask! Most importantly, you need to be yourself—don't try to be something or someone you are not.

RELAY – There is no single correct way to share your faith, but at some point, you need to relay what a relationship with Jesus Christ has done in your life. You should consider sharing a combination of God's Word and your testimony or the testimony of someone you know if your experiences don't relate to the person you are talking to. In listening and asking a question or two, you will usually discover an opportunity to share your testimony – what God has done in your life (1 Peter 3:15). You may even feel inclined to ask permission to share what God's done for you. No one can dispute your testimony, so write it down and know it by heart. Using Scripture phrased as questions ("Did you know that God's Word – the Bible - says in…") helps others see God's plan and sincere love for them and their loved ones.

SCRIPTURES

Some Scriptures (ESV) to share might include:

Romans 3:23, *For all have sinned and fall short of the glory of God.* (ESV)
- Billy Graham once said, "Sin is any thought or action that falls short of God's will." We all have a sinful nature.
- 1 John 5:17 says that: "All unrighteousness is sin."
- You can't save yourself…and no one else can save you except Jesus Christ. How?

Romans 5:8, *…but God shows his love for us in that while we were still sinners, Christ died for us.*"

Rom 6:23, *For the wages of sin is death, but the free gift of God is eternal life in Christ Jesus our Lord.*
- Jesus Christ willingly paid a price for our sins because He was the only one who could.

John 3:16, *For God so loved the world, that he gave his only Son, that whoever believes in him should not perish but have everlasting life.*

- God loves you so much that He allowed His son to die in your place. We do not deserve this free gift of salvation.

2 Corinthians 5:17, *Therefore, if anyone is in Christ, he is a new creation. The old has passed away; Behold, the new has come.*
- Would you like to experience that kind of newness of life?

Romans 10:13, "*For everyone who calls on the name of the Lord will be saved.*"
- When you ask Jesus to forgive you of sin and ask Him to have lordship and leadership of your life, then you are saved! That's called salvation and only God can provide that – it cannot be earned!

WHAT DOES IT MEAN TO "BE SAVED?"

Being *SAVED* is an expression that even Christians find difficult to define. While here on earth, being saved means we have asked God to forgive us of our wrongdoings and to have leadership of our lives. In doing so, we have an advocate or helper in Jesus Christ, who is interceding for us and who has sent His Holy Spirit to help us here on earth. Being *SAVED* also means that when we die, we will spend eternity in the presence of God. The Scripture states that "we shall all stand before the judgment seat of Christ" (Romans 14:10). Being saved involves accepting God's forgiveness for our sins through the work of Jesus Christ on the cross and inviting Jesus Christ to have Lordship and Leadership of our lives (John 14:6). Then, we will avoid, or be *SAVED* from, the eternal damnation or separation from God that comes to those who reject Christ. Remember Romans 6:23 states that the "wages of sin is death." That is a spiritual death which causes a separation from God. Only through Christ's sacrifice on the cross is there forgiveness and the restoring of a right relationship with God.

After sharing your testimony and Scripture is a great time to ask again if you haven't already, "Have you ever had an experience with Jesus

Christ like that?" If they answer "No," you can ask, "Would you like to?" If they avoid the question or get defensive don't worry, just move on and let them know that God loves them and just seemed to nudge you to talk with them about their faith. However, if they say "Yes," you can share a small prayer with them and 2 Corinthians 5:17. The exact wording of the prayer doesn't matter—what matters is the intent of the heart.

PRAYER FOR SALVATION

Dear Jesus, here I am. I'm not perfect; I am a sinner. I ask you to come into my heart and forgive my sins. Please be the Lord of my life; and lead me all the days of my life. In Jesus' name, Amen.

NEVER QUIT – A serious decision that will change your life for eternity is not a decision made lightly, so don't be discouraged and quit if someone doesn't decide for Christ every time you try to share your faith. You must also "earn the right" to speak into someone's life at a spiritual level (which is usually a very guarded place in most people's lives). Sometimes we earn the right when our testimony experience connects with others. But, sometimes earning that right happens over time as we develop trusted relationships with people we care about.

We are all just links in a chain trying to lead others to Christ—no one link is more important than another. God alone knows the heart, and He alone should get all the credit for any good that happens. Survey research indicates that it may take 12 - 15 or more spiritual encounters before someone can make an informed decision for Christ! God has commanded us to scatter the Gospel seed—He will do the rest. As the apostle Paul stated, *"I have planted, Apollos watered; but God gave the increase."* (1 Corinthians 3:6 KJV) So go scatter some seed today!

WHAT'S NEXT?

If you have had the privilege of praying with someone to place their faith in the Lord Jesus Christ, try to give them a Bible or New Testament and encourage them to begin reading it! Many believe that the book of Mark or John may be the best starting point but starting is the key. Also encourage them to attend a good church. Try to get a name and contact information so that you can follow up with them or share the information with your church leadership.

Additionally, you need to share the great things that God is doing in your life as you step out in faith. Sharing the little victories that you experience in talking to other people about what God has done in your life will encourage them. Being honest about fears or insecurities that God has helped you overcome will only bless others who are trying to follow Christ's commands.

Most importantly, you and your friends need to thank the One who allowed you to have divine encounters—God Himself. God alone deserves all the glory for any good that comes of our evangelism efforts. After all, He is the One who sent His Son, Jesus Christ, to take our place on the cross at Calvary. He alone changes hearts. Perhaps today—He has changed yours just a little bit too.

MY PRAYER LIST

I'm praying for (those individuals God has put in your life who do not have a right relationship with God yet):

____

____

____

____

____

____

____

L.E.A.R.N. Evangelism HANDBOOK: Giving Away The Greatest Gift

Join Dr. Windsor as he shares strategies, humorous family stories, and his own faith-sharing adventures to help you see the simplicity of having faith conversations in your everyday life. This engaging resource gives key insights for sharing the greatest gift a Christian has to offer. We all have a story of what God has done in our life, and your story can be THE story that helps change someone else's life for eternity. (225 pp. $14.99 English & Spanish).

L.E.A.R.N. Evangelism: Giving Away The Greatest Gift (pamphlet)

A 28-page pocket-size pamphlet that accompanies the L.E.A.R.N. Evangelism HANDBOOK: Giving Away the Greatest Gift. In just 30 minutes, you will be able to read and reread some simple tips on sharing the hope of Jesus Christ within every Christian. * Available in eBook and paperback versions! ** Discount for wholesale quantities in paperback. Also in Spanish.

Becoming A Spirit-Empowered Evangelist

Ever wonder what evangelist ministry looks like? Do you feel the call to become an evangelist? Becoming A Spirit Empowered Evangelist is a must read for you! Dr. Windsor shares practical insights from over twenty years of ministry and what it takes to stay on the field of ministry. (248 pp. $14.99 English only)

** Visit http://www.learnevangelism.org for more information on these resources and free downloads. Want to plan an evangelism workshop? Send an email to mail@windsmin.org.

RESPONSE FORM

☐ Please send me additional information on becoming a true disciple of Jesus Christ.

☐ Please send me information on quantity discounts for L.E.A.R.N. Evangelism pamphlets to share with my friends, church family, loved ones, and church leaders.

☐ Please send me information on quantity discounts for the book, *L.E.A.R.N. Evangelism Handbook: Giving Away the Greatest Gift* to use in my small group, church teaching series, or personal devotion times.

☐ Please let me know how I can obtain a copy of your book, *Becoming A Spirit Empowered Evangelist*. I truly feel the Lord is dealing with me about discovering more about evangelistic ministry as I pray for other evangelists I know and seek God's direction for my own life.

Name
____

Address
____

City
____

State   Zip
____

Phone

Please call or email any requests to the ministry below. You may also mail response forms (with contact information) in an envelope addressed to (church or ministry contact information providing this resource).

Contact Information:

Luke 10:2, *"And he said to them,
'The harvest is plentiful, but the laborers
are few. Therefore pray earnestly to the Lord
of the Harvest to send out laborers
into his harvest."* (ESV)

http://www.windsmin.org

MY NOTES

MY NOTES

MY NOTES